MATLAB

Programming with MATLAB for Beginners

A Practical Introduction To Programming And Problem Solving

--UpSkill Learning

Dedication

Dedicated to the ones who look at the world from a different perspective, the ones who are restless, the ones who strive for change, the ones who see things differently, the ones who don't accept the status quo, the ones who challenge current thinking patterns, the ones who break down existing barriers, the ones who make the impossible possible, the ones who build new things.....

Copyright

Table Of Contents

Introduction To MATLAB

MATLAB is a programming language developed by MathWorks and it is one of the most important computation languages. The course content covers all the required topics for getting started with MATLAB programming. Imagine having the ability to execute MATLAB commands with ease or create your own functions at will when you're called to solve a problem. In this course, you will master the core MATLAB

Programming skills through instruction and interactive exercises.

We've boiled down the vast amount of information available to deliver exactly what you need to learn to get started in MATLAB. What if you could magically impress your boss with professional graphs or analyze data like a champ? Become that person that your peers call upon when they need help and develop your MATLAB skills to create amazing tools, software, or whatever your heart desires.

MATLAB is a higher level programming language that has various uses in everyday problems. In this book we will first go through the basics needed to begin the start of your programming journey. Such basics include but are not limited to: 1. Assigning numerical values to variables, 2. Manipulating these variables in a meaningful way, 3. Creating and manipulating vectors for problem solving, 4. Creating and manipulating matrices for problem solving, 5. Plotting various graphs to effectively display information.

In this book, you will learn how to program with MATLAB and after you finish this course you can:

- Do basic calculation with MATLAB
- Create variables, vectors and matrices
- Do advanced operations with matrices and vectors
- Create simple and advanced programs to solve your problems
- Plot your data set in 2D and 3D graphs
- Solve algebraic equations and systems
- Solve calculus problems like limits

In this book, we show you each topic step-by-step and you can practice with exercises at the end of the section. After completing this book, you will learn how to:

- Navigate the Environment and Execute Commands with ease
- Create Vectors, Matrices, Arrays and other Variables with confidence
- Perform Operations on large data sets with one command
- Generate professional looking Plots for presentations and documentation

- Automate a group of commands with Scripts and interact with user input
- Develop your own Functions and build MATLAB programs

What are the requirements?

You need a computer with MATLAB

What am I going to get from this course?

- Learn how to use MATLAB and do basic arithmetic
- Programming in MATLAB environment
- Work with variables
- Make 2D and 3D plot
- Create Matrices and do basic and advanced operations
- Work with complex numbers
- Solve equations and system of equations

What is the target audience?

- Engineers, Scientists, and Programmers
- Professionals, Students, & Hobbyists
- MATLAB Programmers looking to refresh their basic skills
- Anyone who wants to master the basic fundamentals of MATLAB

Mastering the basics of MATLAB gives you the ability to learn advanced topics more easily, create amazing tools and software, and conduct engineering tasks with ease. If you want to learn MATLAB for your Work or College, this is the right book for you.

MATLAB Skills For Sculpting Your Career:

Matlab is used in many industries and can essentially be used in any job where data analysis is a desired skill.

As the world becomes more data and statistically driven, many jobs will follow. If you plan to be doing some level of research or data analysis in your career, learning Matlab will be very valuable to you.

You will be able to prototype new ideas quickly and easily. If you are more focused on being a pure software engineer, Matlab may not be the best tool for you. Since it is really aimed more towards scientific computing, it may leave a lot to be desired if you want to develop mobile or web applications.

In general, knowing at least a bit about the environment and language will likely be helpful for the future. At the very least, you will have a good starting point if you find that your career path would include Matlab.

Chapter 1

MATLAB – Intro, Features, Modules & Influence

MATLAB stands for <u>ma</u>trix <u>lab</u>oratory. MATLAB is an environment for multi-paradigm numerical computing. It is a fourth generation programming language.

After reading these statements you might be a little confused about environment, multi-paradigm and numerical computing – but if you think over it a bit, it will be understandable. Let's first consider the environment. What exactly it is? **It is a platform for various programming language with advanced mathematical support.**

MATLAB performs operations on matrix and hence considered for numerical computing. You can use any suitable programming language as per your requirement (depending on the project) or depending on your usage comfortability.

Mathworks developed MATLAB as proprietary programming Language. It not only allows matrix manipulations but also plotting of functions and data, creation of user interface and importantly various algorithms can also be implemented. It supports programs written in other languages, including C, C++, Java, Fortran and Python.

Development of MATLAB started in late 1970s in the University of New Mexico. Mathworks was established in 1984 to continue the development of MATLAB. Later MATLAB was used in many domains.

History

Cleve Moler, the chairman of the computer science department at the University of New Mexico, started developing MATLAB in the late 1970s. He designed it to give his students access to LINPACK and EISPACK without them having to learn Fortran.

It soon spread to other universities and found a strong audience within the applied mathematics community. Jack Little, an engineer, was exposed to it during a visit Moler made to Stanford University in 1983. Recognizing its commercial potential, he joined with Moler and Steve Bangert. They rewrote MATLAB in C and founded MathWorks in 1984 to continue its development. These rewritten libraries were known as JACKPAC. In 2000,

MATLAB was rewritten to use a newer set of libraries for matrix manipulation, LAPACK.

MATLAB was first adopted by researchers and practitioners in control engineering, Little's specialty, but quickly spread to many other domains. It is now also used in education, in particular the teaching of linear algebra, numerical analysis, and is popular amongst scientists involved in image processing.

Features:

- High-level language for scientific and engineering computing
- Desktop environment tuned for iterative exploration, design, and problem-solving
- Graphics for visualizing data and tools for creating custom plots
- Apps for curve fitting, data classification, signal analysis, and many other domain-specific tasks

- Add-on toolboxes for a wide range of engineering and scientific applications

- Tools for building applications with custom user interfaces

Modules

- ✓ Math, Statistics, and Optimization
- ✓ Signal Processing and Communications
- ✓ Control Systems
- ✓ Image Processing and Computer Vision
- ✓ Computational Finance
- ✓ Parallel Computing
- ✓ Application Deployment

Advantages of Using MATLAB:

MATLAB has several advantages over other methods or languages.

- Its basic data element is the matrix. A simple integer is considered a matrix of one row and one column. Several mathematical operations that work on arrays or matrices are built-in to the Matlab environment. For example, cross-products, dot-products, determinants, inverse matrices.

- Vectorized operations. Adding two arrays together needs only one command, instead of a *for or while loop*.

- The graphical output is optimized for interaction. You can plot your data very easily, and then change colors, sizes, scales, etc, by using the graphical interactive tools.

- Matlab's functionality can be greatly expanded by the addition of toolboxes. These are sets of specific functions that provided more specialized functionality. Ex: Excel link allows data to be written in a format recognized by Excel, Statistics Toolbox allows more specialized statistical manipulation of data (Anova, Basic Fits, etc)

- Matlab is not only a programming language, but a programming environment as well.

- You can perform operations from the command line, as a sophisticated calculator or you can create programs and functions that perform repetitive tasks, just as any other computer language.

Influence of MATLAB on various fields:

MATLAB has influence over many areas of human technology from Artificial Intelligence to Aerospace. MATLAB has help and demo projects on various domains and tools. This help and demo is internally available in MATLAB. It has influence on Mathematics and many control systems, RF systems etc.

The above mentioned is MATLAB influence is just the tip of the iceberg, to learn more about what you can do with MATLAB, open your MATLAB software → to the bottom left of your screen you will see a start button → Click on it and go to Toolboxes a new menu will pop up. These are the various tools that MATLAB has to offer.

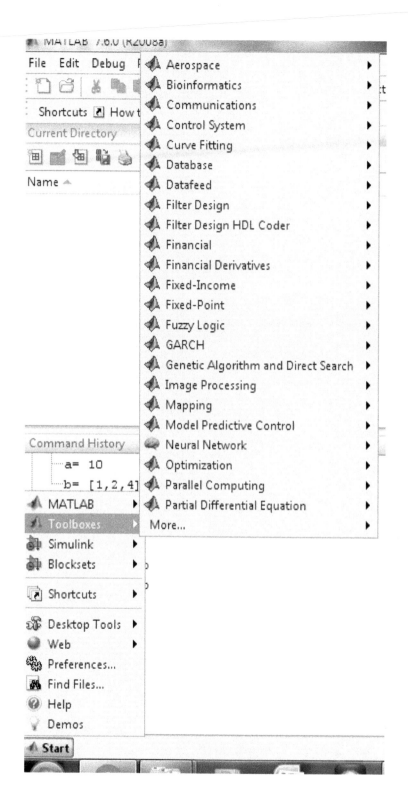

Chapter 2

Getting started with MATLAB

As discussed in the earlier chapter we can conclude that MATLAB is not only a programming language but also an advanced platform for many domains. To program in MATLAB, we must first be familiar with **its work environment, its user interface and its tools**. This chapter will help you to understand the exact structure of MATLAB. It will guide you through the various windows, their usage and significance.

When you open your MATLAB software you will see the following image. Now you can see that there are many windows and it is essential that you need to get introduced to them.

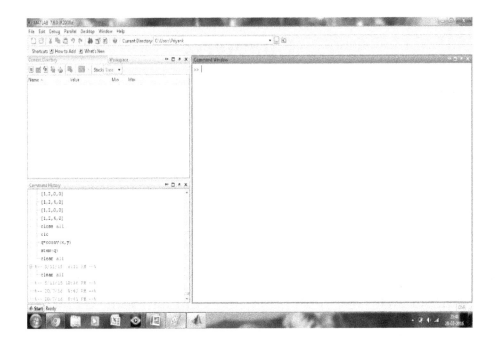

In this chapter, we will learn step by step to get familiar with all the windows and their functionality. These windows include command window, workspace, command history and Current directory. Let's get started with the current directory window.

Current Directory

Current directory window displays the current directory of your project. It shows you the folder in which your current project is going on. It also helps in keeping track of previously made files and projects.

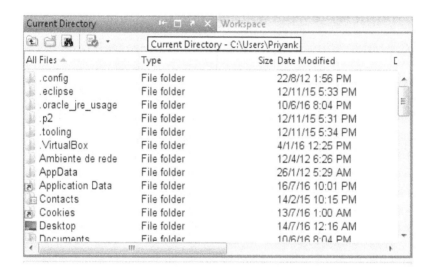

If you notice the Current directory window and Workspace window have shared their places so only one can remain active at a time for display. But if you want you can simply separate out any window by just clicking it and dragging it out.

Command Window

Command window is to give real time commands on the go. If you observe you will always see a double " >> " symbol at the start of every line on command line. This window is used to give commands to MATLAB in more generalized sense like close all, clear all and quit etc. so the quit command will close and exit MATLAB.

You can assign values to variables in command window. These variables will be available in MATLAB for further operations until you remove them.

```
Command Window
>> a= 10

a =

    10

>> b= [1,2,4]

b =

    1    2    4

>>
```

Workspace

Workspace shows all the variables that have been initialized in MATLAB. Workspace stores everything in the form of matrix. This is because MATLAB understands only in terms of Matrix. Thus it saves them as Matrix. As in above example we have initialized a and b. which will show up in Workspace.

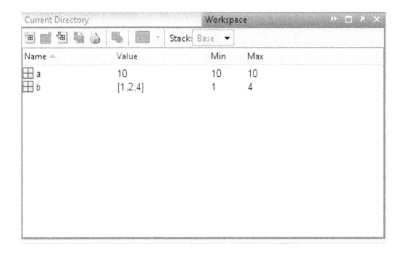

You can directly add the variables in workspace which will be accessible from command window. Workspace allows you to print the variables, generate new ones as well as Import them from some other directory.

Command History

Command history shows the coomands that have been used. This helps to keep track off our commands and their respective outcomes along with time. For example we have initialized variables a and b, commands for these have be reflected in Command History.

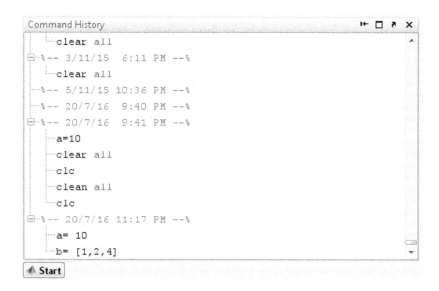

These are the default windows in MATLAB, but the main window that hosts these windows has few functions. We will go through these functions one-by-one.

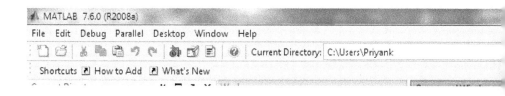

It shows options like File, Edit, Debug, Parallel Desktop, Window and Help along with these it shows new file, cut, copy, paste, undo and redo functionality. You can also verify your current directory from this Tab. Let's explore the various options available in each **options**.

File:

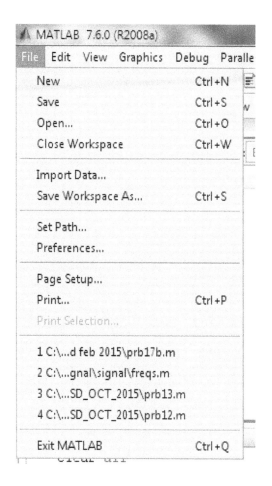

The file provides various options like new, save open close Workspace, along with their quick access keys. It also shows your recent projects and files. It also gives options for Exiting MATLAB.

Edit:

Edit shows all the standard options that are available in any writing tool. It also provides options like clearing command history, command windows and workspace. As for now these few options are more than enough we will slowly explore the remaining options as we learn further concepts.

Chapter 3

Getting familiar with MATLAB

To get familiar with MATLAB we will start with some basic operations. Let's start with simple math operations like addition, subtraction, multiplication and a few others. In simple terms we will be using MATLAB as a calculator. We will directly perform operations using command window.

We will start with initializing 3 variables a, b, Ans. To initialize these variables on command window type as follows.

```
>> a = 10
>> b = 20
>> Ans = a+b
```

You will see the results as shown below:

Command window:

```
Command Window
>> a = 10

a =

    10

>> b = 20

b =

    20

>> Ans = a + b

Ans =

    30

>>
```

Workspace:

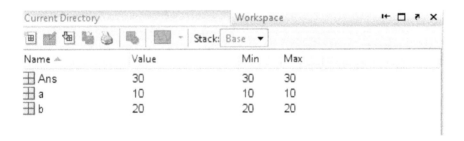

As soon as we enter any command MATLAB responds to it and gives us a feedback message, in our case when we enter **a and its value**. MATLAB responds by sending the same on screen. And the same entries are made in workspace.

Subtraction:

Now once we have done initialization of variables we can again use them directly. To perform subtraction we simply need to enter the following command.

$$>> \text{Ans} = a - b$$

```
Command Window
>> a = 10

a =

    10
>> b = 20

b =

    20
>> Ans = a + b

Ans =

    30
>> Ans = a - b

Ans =

    -10
```

Workspace:

Name ▲	Value	Min	Max
Ans	-10	-10	-10
a	10	10	10
b	20	20	20

Current Directory | Workspace

Stack: Base ▼

Multiplication:

As with all the other programming language, the symbol for multiplication is '*'. Now we will not use our variable **Ans** to store answer, instead we will simply enter the following command and see what happens.

a*b

```
Command Window
>> a*b

ans =

    200

>> |
```

You can see MATLAB has provided us with a new variable **ans.** A new entry in Workspace has been made for it automatically.

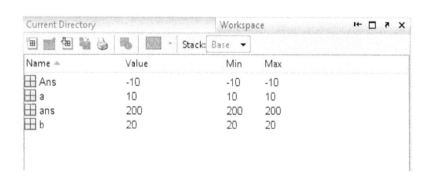

```
Current Directory                    Workspace          I← □ ↗ ×
 ▦ ▦ ▦ ▦ ▦   ▦   ▦  ▾  Stack: Base ▾
Name ▲          Value            Min      Max
▦ Ans           -10              -10      -10
▦ a             10               10       10
▦ ans           200              200      200
▦ b             20               20       20
```

Division:

Our general symbol for division is ' / ' , we going to enter the following command

a / b

and like the previous example you will see the result. It gives **ans** as 0.5000, this is because MATLAB by default takes variables as double.

Command Window
```
>> a/b

ans =

    0.5000

>>
```

Name ▲	Value	Min	Max
Ans	-10	-10	-10
a	10	10	10
ans	0.5000	0.5000	0.5000
b	20	20	20

Current Directory   Workspace

Stack: Base ▼

MATLAB by default displays only 4 decimals in the result of the calculations, for example 0.5000, as shown in above examples. However, MATLAB does numerical calculations in double precision, which is 15 digits. The command format controls how the results of computations are displayed.

Syntax:

>> format short

>>format long

There is one more way to edit variables.

You can double click on variables in workspace.

A new window will open, shrinking the command window.

As shown in the image bellow

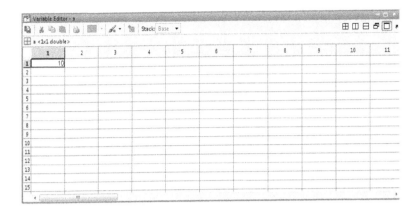

Here you will see it as Microsoft excel sheet, but in fact it is matrix so every cell represents a element of matrix. Just enter the value that you want for that variable and it will be changed.

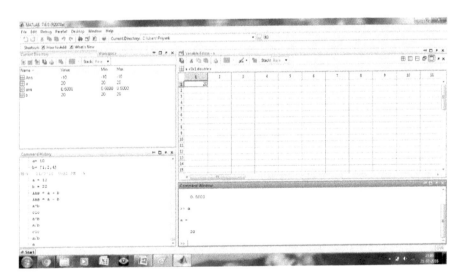

Chapter 4

Basic Commands in MATLAB

Now that we have finished with simple math operations let's move towards learning a few more commands of MATLAB. MATLAB is designed in such a way that it can very well guide you to use any of its command.

But how to use this MATLAB feature?

MATLAB provides a **help browser** which provides you help even offline. It has documentation on every command in MATLAB along with examples.

To use this browser click on HELP on the uppermost tool bar on your default window.

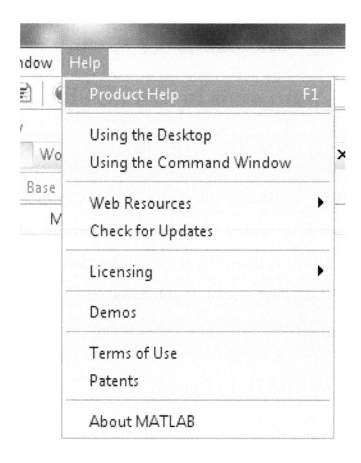

Once you click on the **product help** a new window will pop as shown in the following image.

You can see the detailed document or the **Help Links** regarding 'your doubt/query' in the right side of window. And on the left side you will be able to see all the various tools and modules in MATLAB.

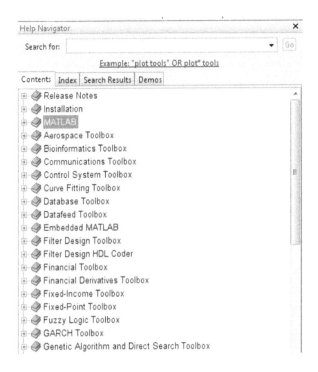

Even if you don't know any of the command you can traverse through the list of appropriate modules and find any command you desire. But if you know the name of the command but you don't know its exact and detailed function you can go for an alternate method that is using help from command window. MATLAB has provided a complete document on "Help".

Just enter the following command on command window.

Help help

Once you hit enter you will get a brief guide on using help.

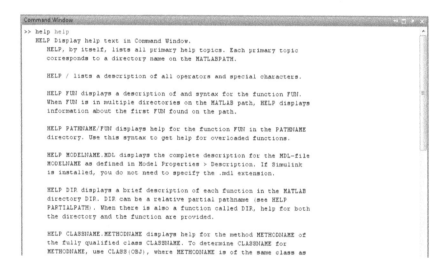

In similar way just type help and command name in front of it and short document will appear in command window.

E.g.:

Help clc

This will display help on clc command.

Clear

As the name suggests, it **clears.** But what it clears?

CLEAR removes all variables from the workspace.

CLEAR VARIABLES does the same thing.

CLEAR GLOBAL removes all global variables.

CLEAR FUNCTIONS removes all compiled M- and MEX-functions

CLEAR ALL removes all variables, globals, functions and MEX links.

You just need to type

Clear all   *change all with desired type

First we initialized a few variables and we could see them in work space.

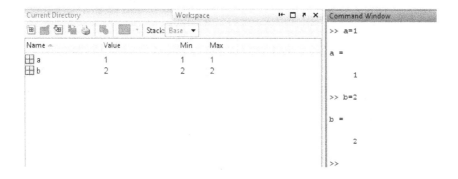

As soon as we enter clear all workspace will be cleared thus the variables a and b will not exist anymore. But command window will continue to show our previous commands.

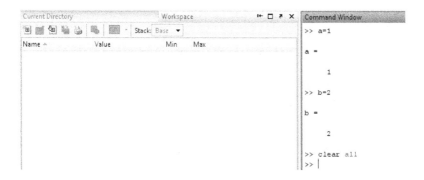

Close

Close indicates to close certain window. Now what is the need of this close command when we have close buttons for every window. Well the use is when we run a project with many windows, especially figure windows, it is easy to mention in the program itself to close windows or manually enter only one command instead of closing all windows manually.

CLOSE(H) closes the window with handle H.

CLOSE, by itself, closes the current figure window.

CLOSE('name') closes the named window.

CLOSE ALL closes all the open figure windows.

CLOSE ALL HIDDEN closes hidden windows as well.

STATUS = CLOSE(...) returns 1 if the specified windows were closed and 0 otherwise.

e.g.:

>> close all

It will close all the figure windows.

CLC:

A very simple command "clc" which clears the command window. But it does not affect workspace or command history. All the variables and function are as they were.

Syntax :

>>clc

We will again initialize variable a and then demonstrate the clc command.

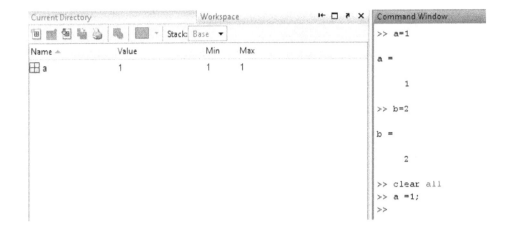

After we enter our command, **command window** will be clear but workspace is not affected. We can still use "a".

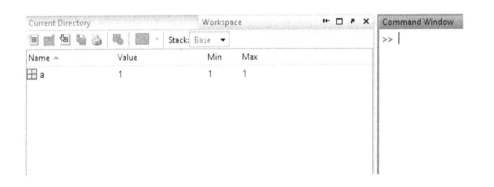

Who

The command shows variable along with their size and type. You just need to enter **who** to display all your variables. If you want to know details of any variable enter 'whos' and variable name.

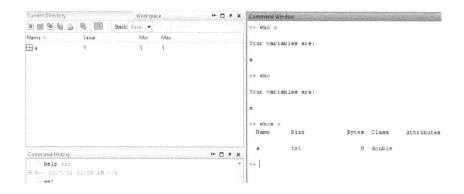

Chapter 5

Matrix Operations

In MATLAB every variable is treated as matrix. So it is important to learn operations on matrix which will help us utilize MATLAB in more efficient way.

A matrix is a two-dimensional array consisting of m rows and n columns. Special cases are column vectors (n = 1) and row vectors (m = 1).

A matrix is an array of numbers. To type a matrix into MATLAB you must

[1] begin with a square bracket, [

[2] separate elements in a row with spaces or commas (,)

[3] use a semicolon (;) to separate rows

[4] end the matrix with another square bracket,]

E.g:

a = [10, 20; 40, 50; 70, 80]

Now we will see the size of our matrix using 'whos' command

```
a =

    10    20
    40    50
    70    80

>> whos a
  Name        Size            Bytes  Class      Attributes

  a           3x2                48  double
```

Once we have entered the matrix, it is automatically stored and remembered in the Workspace. We can refer to it simply as matrix A. The element of row *i* and column *j* of the matrix A is denoted by A(i,j). Thus, A(i,j) in MATLAB refers to the element Aij of matrix A. The ⁻rst index is the row number and the second index is the column number.

For example, A(1,3) is an element of ¯rst row and third column. We can then view a particular element in a matrix by specifying its location

E.g.:

>> a(1,2)

It will give element of 2nd column of 1st row.

Current Directory				Workspace		Command Window
圕 圈 圈 圌 昌 圖 ▾ Stack: Base ▾						>> a(1,2)
Name ▲	Value		Min	Max		ans =
a	[10,20;40,50;70,80]		10	80		
ans	20		20	20		20
						>>

This was the most straight forward way of entering elements in matrix but there many more ways that can be used to enter elements in a matrix in MATLAB.

Colon operator

The colon operator will prove very useful and understanding how it works is the key to efficient and convenient usage of MATLAB.

It occurs in several different forms. Often we must deal with matrices or vectors that are too large to enter one element at a time. For example, suppose we want to enter a **vector a** consisting of values of time from 0 to 1 at interval of 0.01 this operator comes in handy.

(0; 0.01; 0.02; 0.03;   ;1). We can use the command

>> a = 0:0.01:1;

The row vector has 101 elements.

Colon operator in a matrix

The colon operator can also be used to pick out a certain row or column. For example, the statement A(m:n,k:l) specifies rows m to n and column k to l. Subscript expressions refer to portions of a matrix.

For example,

>> a(2,:)

ans =

40 50

is the second row elements of a.

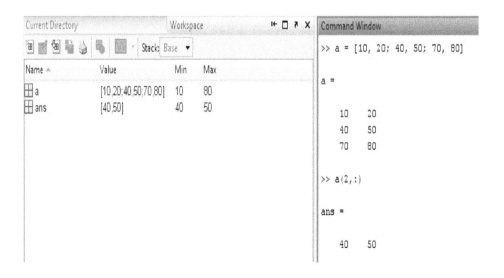

Linear spacing

On the other hand, there is a command to generate linearly spaced matrix: **linspace**. It is similar to the colon operator (:), but gives direct control over the number of points.

For example,

b = linspace(x,y)

This generates a row vector b of 100 points linearly spaced between and including x and y.

b = linspace(x,y,n)

This generates a row vector y of n points linearly spaced between and including x and y. This is useful when we want to divide an interval into a number of subintervals of the same length.

For example,

>> theta = linspace(0,2*pi,10)

Dimension

To determine the dimensions of a matrix or vector, use the command size.

For example,

>> size(a)

ans =

    1   10

means 3 rows and 3 columns.

Now that we have studied how to enter a matrix in MATLAB, we can move to performing operations on matrix.

Transposing a matrix

The transpose operation is denoted by an apostrophe or a single quote ('). It flips a matrix about its main diagonal and it turns a row vector into a column vector. Thus,

>> a'

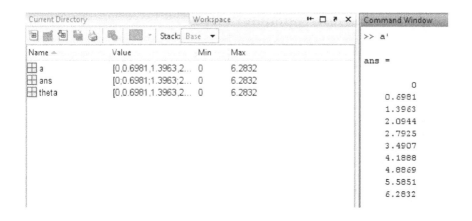

By using linear algebra notation, the transpose of m X n real matrix A is the n X m matrix that results from interchanging the rows and columns of A. The transpose matrix is denoted AT.

Concatenating matrices

Matrices can be made up of sub-matrices. Here is an example. First, generate a matrix a

A =

1 2 3

4 5 6

7 8 9

The new matrix B will be,

>> B = [A 10*A; -A [1 0 0; 0 1 0; 0 0 1]]

Current Directory	Workspace			Command Window

```
>> b=[A 10*A; -A [1 0 0; 0 1 0; 0 0 1]]

b =

    1     2     3    10    20    30
    4     5     6    40    50    60
    7     8     9    70    80    90
   -1    -2    -3     1     0     0
   -4    -5    -6     0     1     0
   -7    -8    -9     0     0     1

>>
```

Workspace:

Name	Value	Min	Max
A	[1,2,3;4,5,6;7,8,9]	1	9
b	<6x6 double>	-9	90

Matrix generators:

Matrix generator functions of MATLAB provide an option for generation variety of matrices. These options range from Identity matrix, ones matrix to zero matrix and so on. We will one by one study these functions.

eye(m,n)

This function returns an m-by-n matrix with 1 on the main diagonal.

eye(n)

It returns an n-by-n square identity matrix

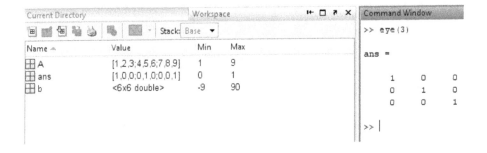

zeros(m,n)

this function returns an m-by-n matrix of zeros. I.e. all the elements of this matrix will be zero

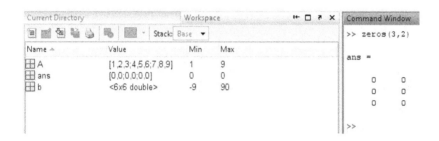

ones(m,n)

As the name indicates it returns an m-by-n matrix of ones. All the elements in this matrix are '1'.

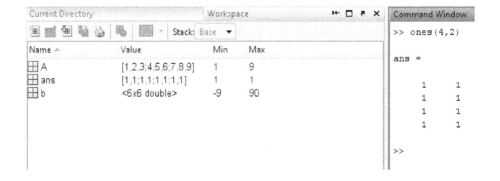

diag(A)

This function is used to extract the diagonal of matrix A. this plays a lot of significance in operations on matrices.

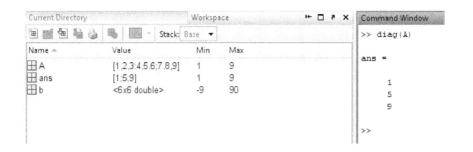

rand(m,n)

It returns an m-by-n matrix of random numbers

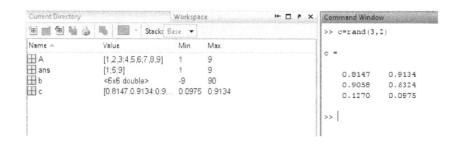

det

syntax :

c= det(a)

This returns the determinant of the square matrix

eig

Eigenvalues and eigenvectors

[V,D] = EIG(X) produces a diagonal matrix D of eigenvalues and a full matrix V whose columns are the corresponding eigenvectors so that X*V = V*D

inv

Matrix inverse

INV(X) is the inverse of the square matrix X. A warning message is printed if X is badly scaled or nearly singular.

norm

Matrix and vector norms

For matrices...

NORM(X) is the largest singular value of X, max(svd(X)).

NORM(X,2) is the same as NORM(X).

NORM(X,1) is the 1-norm of X, the largest column sum,

$$= \text{max(sum(abs(X))).}$$

NORM(X,inf) is the infinity norm of X, the largest row sum,

$$= \text{max(sum(abs(X'))).}$$

NORM(X,'fro') is the Frobenius norm, sqrt(sum(diag(X'*X))).

NORM(X,P) is available for matrix X only if P is 1, 2, inf or 'fro'.

For vectors...

$NORM(V,P) = sum(abs(V).^P)^(1/P).$

$NORM(V) = norm(V,2).$

$NORM(V,inf) = max(abs(V)).$

$NORM(V,-inf) = min(abs(V)).$

rank

Number of linearly independent rows or columns

RANK(A) provides an estimate of the number of linearly independent rows or columns of a matrix A.

RANK(A,tol) is the number of singular values of A that are larger than tol.

cond

Condition number with respect to inversion.

COND(X) returns the 2-norm condition number (the ratio of the largest singular value of X to the smallest). Large condition numbers indicate a nearly singular matrix.

COND(X,P) returns the condition number of X in P-norm:

NORM(X,P) * NORM(INV(X),P).

where P = 1, 2, inf, or 'fro'.

Chapter 6

Array and Linear Operations

MATLAB has two different types of arithmetic operations: **matrix arithmetic operations** and **array arithmetic operations**. Array arithmetic operations or array operations are done element-by-element. The period character, ., distinguishes the array operations from the matrix operations. However, since the matrix and array operations are the same for addition (+) and subtraction (-), the character pairs (.+) and (.-) are not used. The list of array operators are shown below. If A and B are two matrices of the same size with elements A = [aij] and B = [bij], then the command

.*   Element-by-element multiplication

./   Element-by-element division

.^   Element-by-element exponentiation

>> C = A.*B

This produces another matrix C of the same size with elements [cij] = [aij][bij] . For example, using the same 3 X 3 matrices,

A =

    1 2 3

    4 5 6

    7 8 9

B =

    10 20 30

    40 50 60

    70 80 90

We have,

>> C = A.*B

C =

10 40 90

160 250 360

490 640 810

To raise a scalar to a power, we use for example the command 10^2. If we want the operation to be applied to each element of a matrix, we use .^2. For example, if we want to produce a new matrix whose elements are the square of the elements of the matrix A, we enter

>> A.^2

ans =

1 4 9

16 25 36

49 64 81

The relations below summarize the above operations. To simplify, let's consider two vectors U and V with elements U = [ui] and V = [vj].

U: * V produces [u1v1 u2v2 : : : unvn]

U:/V produces [u1/v1 u2/v2 : : : un/vn]

Operation	Matrix	Array
Addition	+	+
Subtraction	-	-
Multiplication	*	.*
Division	/	./
Left division	\	.\
Exponentiation	^	.^

In mathematics or most of the fundamental science calculations linear equations play a very vital role. Sometimes it is very difficult to solve them by our regular method. Then we opt for **Cramer's rule,** i.e. using matrix.

For example:

$$x + 2y + 3z = 1$$

$$4x + 5y + 6z = 1$$

$$7x + 8y = 1$$

The coefficient matrix A is

A =

1 2 3

4 5 6

7 8 9

And the vector b =

1

1

1

With matrix notation, a system of simultaneous linear equations is written

$$Ax = b$$

This equation can be solved for x using linear algebra. The result is $x = A^{-1}b$.

There are typically two ways to solve for **x** in MATLAB:

1. The first one is to use the matrix inverse, inv.

>> A = [1 2 3; 4 5 6; 7 8 0];

>> b = [1; 1; 1];

>> x = inv(A)*b

x =

-1.0000

1.0000

-0.0000

2. The second one is to use the backslash (\)operator. The numerical algorithm behind this operator is computationally efficient. This is a numerically reliable way of solving system of linear equations by using a well-known process of Gaussian elimination.

>> A = [1 2 3; 4 5 6; 7 8 0];

>> b = [1; 1; 1];

>> x = A\b

x =

-1.0000

1.0000

-0.0000

This problem is at the heart of many problems in scientific computation. Hence it is important that we know how to solve this type of problem efficiently.

Now, we know how to solve a system of linear equations.

Chapter 7

Programming with MATLAB

In the above chapters, we've learned all the commands that are entered from command window. But programs cannot be written on command window. The commands on command window cannot be saved for later use so this is definitely not the way to write programs in MATLAB.

A different way of executing commands with MATLAB is:

1. **To create a file with a list of commands,**
2. **Save the file, and**
3. **Run the file.**

Files used in MATLAB programming are called as **script**. Scripts are the simplest kind of M-file. They are useful for automating blocks of MATLAB commands, such as

computations you have to perform repeatedly from the command line.

Scripts can operate on existing data in the workspace, or they can create new data on which to operate. Although scripts do not return output arguments, any variables that they create remain in the workspace, so you can use them in further computations.

In addition, scripts can produce graphical output using commands like plot. Script files have a filename extension of **.m** and are often called M-files. To write a script or M-file we need editor. To start an editor we have two ways, using GUI of MATLAB or using command line interface.

Using GUI ->file

->new

->M-file

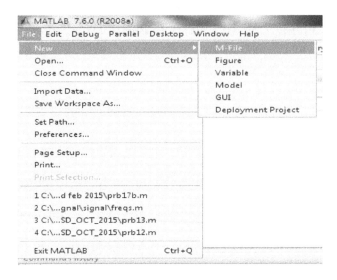

For this function, MATLAB has provided a quick access button on the main screen.

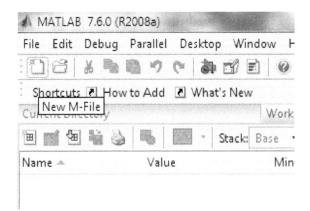

Using command window enter following command

>>edit

Or

>>edit filename.m

The editor window looks like following:

Let us create a file which will plot a **sine wave**. You may just copy and paste the program as it is as we are to study many functions and commands.

x = 0:pi/100:2*pi;

y = cos(x);

plot(x,y)

ylabel('Cosine functions')

legend('cos(x)')

title('example M-file')

axis([0 2*pi -3 3])

Once you have copied this program in editor press "ctrl+s" or go to file → click on save. Save your file in desired location. A new window to save will pop up.

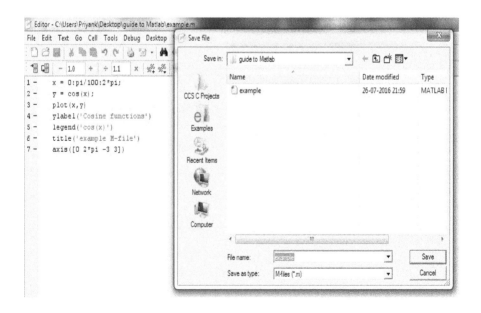

Once you have saved it, you are ready to run it. To run file click on the button as shown in the image below:

MATLAB will take some time to give the output depending on your system configuration and you will be able to see the following output.

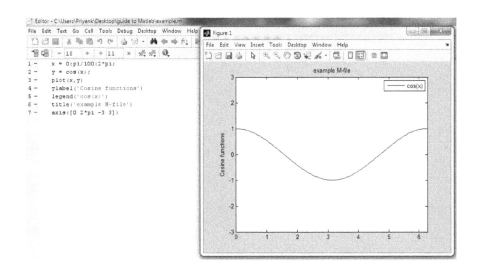

M files can be of two types: they can be simple scripts or functions. For now we have discussed only the script ones but once we get hold of MATALB and script we will find it very easy to generate a function file.

Chapter 8

Input, Output and Operators

Now that we have learned about script files we must also know how to give inputs to a file and how to get outputs. Let's get started learning the input, output and operators.

Input command:

To give input MATLAB has given special command as "Input". Input is used to request user input.

Syntax

user_entry = input('prompt')

user_entry = input('prompt', 's')

Description

The response to the input prompt can be any MATLAB expression, which is evaluated using the variables in the current workspace.

user_entry = input('prompt') displays prompt as a prompt on the screen, waits for input from the keyboard, and returns the value entered in user_entry.

user_entry = input('prompt', 's') returns the entered string as a text variable rather than as a variable name or numerical value.

Note: if the user simply hits the **return (enter)** key then an empty matrix is returned. Also MATLAB will keep receiving input until return key is pressed.

E.g.:

number = input('enter the number whose square you want :')

sqr_num = number*number;

disp(sqr_num)

Output commands:

Inputs are important but so are the outputs. Many a times we are required to display our results or responses. There are few commands that MATLAB provides. They are listed below:

1. **disp**
2. **fprintf**

disp:

disp is used to simply display values or string in a very blind way. It does not allow users to manipulate the way in which it will display.

Syntax

disp(X)

Description

disp(X) displays an array, without printing the array name. If X contains a text string, the string is displayed.

Another way to display an array on the screen is to type its name, but this prints a leading "X=," which is not always desirable.

Note: disp does not display empty arrays

E.g.:

number = input('enter the number whose square you want :')

sqr_num = number*number;

disp('square of the number you entered is: ')

disp(sqr_num)

fprintf:

fprintf is relatively complex command than disp. Where disp only displays on output screen fprintf can also be used to write to a file. It provides various options as how long or how precise the value to be displayed will etc.

Syntax

count = fprintf(fid, format, A, ...)

Description

count = fprintf(fid, format, A, ...) formats the data in the real part of matrix A (and in any additional matrix arguments) under control of the specified format string, and writes it to the file associated with file identifier fid. fprintf returns a count of the number of bytes written.

Argument fid is an integer file identifier obtained from fopen. (It can also be 1 for standard output (the screen) or 2 for standard error.) Omitting fid causes output to appear on the screen.

Format String

The format argument is a string containing ordinary characters and/or C language conversion specifications. A conversion specification controls the notation, alignment, significant digits, field width, and other aspects of output format. The format string can contain escape characters to represent nonprinting characters such as newline characters and tabs.

E.g.:

fprintf(1,'hello.\n')

fprintf('world')

Note: be careful while coping fprintf statements in MATLAB always remember to change the inverted commas the one in doc is not accepted by MATLAB.

Operators:

Relational and logical operators

A relational operator compares two numbers by determining whether a comparison is true or false. Relational operators are listed below.

>	Greater than
<	Less than
>=	Greater than or equal to
<=	Less than or equal to
==	Equal to
~=	Not equal to
&	AND operator
|	OR operator
~	NOT operator

Operator precedence

We can build expressions that use any combination of arithmetic, relational, and logical operators. Precedence rules determine the order in which MATLAB evaluates an expression.

The precedence rules for MATLAB are shown in this list, ordered from highest to lowest precedence level. Operators are evaluated from left to right.

Precedence Operator

1. 1 Parentheses ()
2. 2 Transpose (.'), power (.^), matrix power (^)
3. 3 Unary plus (+), unary minus (-), logical negation (~)
4. 4 Multiplication (.*), right division (./), left division (.\),matrix multiplication (*), matrix right   division (/), matrix left division (\)

5. 5 Addition (+), subtraction (-)

6. 6 Colon operator (:)

7. 7 Less than (<), less than or equal to (<=), greater (>), greater than or equal to (>=), equal to (==), not equal to (~=)

8. 8 Element-wise AND, (&)

9. 9 Element-wise OR, (|)

Chapter 9

Flow Control Statements

Flow control statements play a vital role in developing any program. They provide you with control in program runtime. We can decide what program should perform in different cases or situations. We will be studying such statements in following chapter.

IF – ELSE

Execute statements if condition is true. Only if statement can be used it is not mandatory to use else or elseif.

Syntax

if expression, statements, end

Description

if expression, statements, end evaluates expression and, if the evaluation yields logical 1 (true) or a nonzero result, executes one or more MATLAB® commands denoted here as statements.

if expression1

    statements1

elseif expression2

    statements2

else

    statements3

end

Example:

a=10,b=5;

if(a>b)

disp(a)

else

disp(b)

end

flow control statements can also be used to run certain statements for number of times. For such implementation we can use for.

For

Execute block of code specified number of times

Syntax

for x=initval:endval, statements, end

for x=initval:stepval:endval, statements, end

Description

for x=initval:endval, statements, end repeatedly executes one or more MATLAB statements in a loop. Loop counter variable x is initialized to value initval at the start of the first pass through the loop, and automatically increments by 1 each time through the loop.

The program makes repeated passes through statements until either x has incremented to the value endval, or MATLAB encounters a break, or return instruction, thus forcing an immediately exit of the loop. If MATLAB encounters a continue statement in the loop code, it immediately exits the current pass at the location of the continue statement, skipping any remaining code in that pass, and begins another pass at the start of the loop statements with the value of the loop counter incremented by 1.

The values initval and endval must be real numbers or arrays of real numbers, or can also be calls to functions that return the same. The value assigned to x is often used in the code within the loop, however it is recommended that you do not assign to x in the loop code.

for x=initval:stepval:endval, statements, end is the same as the above syntax, except that loop counter x is incremented (or decremented when stepval is negative) by the value stepval on each iteration through the loop. The value stepval must be a real number or can also be a call to a function that returns a real number.

for variable = initval:endval

    statement

    ...

    statement

end

example:

disp('table of two upto 10')

for x= 1:10

```
a=2*x;

disp(a)

end
```

while

Repeatedly execute statements while condition is true

Syntax

while expression, statements, end

Description

while expression, statements, end repeatedly executes one or more MATLAB® statements in a loop, continuing until expression no longer holds true or until MATLAB encounters a break, or return instruction. thus forcing an immediately exit of the loop. If MATLAB encounters a continue statement in the loop code, it immediately exits the current pass at the location of the continue statement, skipping any remaining code in that pass, and begins another pass at the start of the loop statements with the value of the loop counter incremented by 1.

expression is a MATLAB expression that evaluates to a result of logical 1 (true) or logical 0 (false). expression can be scalar or an array. It must contain all real elements, and the statement all(A(:)) must be equal to logical 1 for the expression to be true.

A = 0;

while A<10

disp(A)

A=A+1;

end

The above function will print A from 0 to 9.

Note: while performing operations using while or any conditional flow statements you might get struck in infinite loop. Use "Ctrl + C".

Chapter 10

Math Functions

As we discussed earlier MATLAB was designed for many mathematical operations using computer. To cater the needs for mathematical calculations MATLAB provides many inbuilt function. These functions range from trigonometry to logarithms. To get the list of all the function you can either go through the list below or use MATLAB help feature. To get help from MATLAB you have to enter the following command on command window.

>>help elfun

This will display all the elementary functions

or

>>help specfun

This will display special math functions.

List of all the elementary functions

Trigonometric.

sin   - Sine.

sind   - Sine of argument in degrees.

sinh   - Hyperbolic sine.

asin   - Inverse sine.

asind   - Inverse sine, result in degrees.

asinh   - Inverse hyperbolic sine.

cos   - Cosine.

cosd   - Cosine of argument in degrees.

cosh   - Hyperbolic cosine.

acos   - Inverse cosine.

acosd   - Inverse cosine, result in degrees.

acosh   - Inverse hyperbolic cosine.

tan   - Tangent.

tand   - Tangent of argument in degrees.

tanh   - Hyperbolic tangent.

atan   - Inverse tangent.

atand   - Inverse tangent, result in degrees.

atan2   - Four quadrant inverse tangent.

atanh   - Inverse hyperbolic tangent.

sec   - Secant.

secd   - Secant of argument in degrees.

sech   - Hyperbolic secant.

asec   - Inverse secant.

asecd   - Inverse secant, result in degrees.

asech   - Inverse hyperbolic secant.

csc   - Cosecant.

cscd   - Cosecant of argument in degrees.

csch   - Hyperbolic cosecant.

acsc   - Inverse cosecant.

acscd   - Inverse cosecant, result in degrees.

acsch   - Inverse hyperbolic cosecant.

cot   - Cotangent.

cotd   - Cotangent of argument in degrees.

coth   - Hyperbolic cotangent.

acot   - Inverse cotangent.

acotd   - Inverse cotangent, result in degrees.

acoth   - Inverse hyperbolic cotangent.

hypot   - Square root of sum of squares.

Exponential.

exp   - Exponential.

expm1   - Compute exp(x)-1 accurately.

log   - Natural logarithm.

log1p   - Compute log(1+x) accurately.

log10   - Common (base 10) logarithm.

log2   - Base 2 logarithm and dissect floating point number.

pow2   - Base 2 power and scale floating point number.

realpow - Power that will error out on complex result.

reallog - Natural logarithm of real number.

realsqrt - Square root of number greater than or equal to zero.

sqrt   - Square root.

nthroot - Real n-th root of real numbers.

nextpow2 - Next higher power of 2.

Complex.

abs   - Absolute value.

angle   - Phase angle.

complex   - Construct complex data from real and imaginary parts.

conj   - Complex conjugate.

imag   - Complex imaginary part.

real   - Complex real part.

unwrap   - Unwrap phase angle.

isreal   - True for real array.

cplxpair   - Sort numbers into complex conjugate pairs.

Rounding and remainder.

fix   - Round towards zero.

floor   - Round towards minus infinity.

ceil   - Round towards plus infinity.

round   - Round towards nearest integer.

mod   - Modulus (signed remainder after division).

rem   - Remainder after division.

sign   - Signum.

List of the special functions is stated as bellow.

Specialized math functions.

airy   - Airy functions.

besselj   - Bessel function of the first kind.

bessely   - Bessel function of the second kind.

besselh   - Bessel functions of the third kind (Hankel function).

besseli   - Modified Bessel function of the first kind.

besselk   - Modified Bessel function of the second kind.

beta   - Beta function.

betainc   - Incomplete beta function.

betaln   - Logarithm of beta function.

ellipj   - Jacobi elliptic functions.

ellipke   - Complete elliptic integral.

erf   - Error function.

erfc   - Complementary error function.

erfcx   - Scaled complementary error function.

erfinv   - Inverse error function.

expint   - Exponential integral function.

gamma   - Gamma function.

gammainc   - Incomplete gamma function.

gammaln   - Logarithm of gamma function.

psi   - Psi (polygamma) function.

legendre   - Associated Legendre function.

cross   - Vector cross product.

dot   - Vector dot product.

Number theoretic functions.

factor   - Prime factors.

isprime   - True for prime numbers.

primes   - Generate list of prime numbers.

gcd   - Greatest common divisor.

lcm   - Least common multiple.

rat   - Rational approximation.

rats   - Rational output.

perms   - All possible permutations.

nchoosek   - All combinations of N elements taken K at a time.

factorial - Factorial function.

Coordinate transforms.

cart2sph   - Transform Cartesian to spherical coordinates.

cart2pol   - Transform Cartesian to polar coordinates.

pol2cart   - Transform polar to Cartesian coordinates.

sph2cart   - Transform spherical to Cartesian coordinates.

hsv2rgb   - Convert hue-saturation-value colors to red-green-blue.

rgb2hsv   - Convert red-green-blue colors to hue-saturation-value.

The detail of every function is difficult to mention in this document so we will be just listing them. Once you go through the list, you can get an idea about all the internal function that we can use.

Sin

Sine of argument in radians

Syntax

$Y = \sin(X)$

Description

The sin function operates element-wise on arrays. The function's domains and ranges include complex values. All angles are in radians.

$Y = \sin(X)$ returns the circular sine of the elements of X

This was about sine but we have made short list that we can always need.

$\cos(x)$ Cosine

$\sin(x)$ Sine

Chapter 11

Strings

What are "strings"? MATLAB defines strings as "a vector whose components are the numeric codes for the characters".

Various operations can be performed on strings. But these operations require different functions. In many languages we need to develop logic for these operations. But MATLAB has provided inbuilt functions that help us. This allows us to focus on our actual implementation and we need not spend our time on deciding logics for operations.

Lets us first start with handling of strings:

Syntax and description

S = 'Any Characters'

S = 'Any Characters' creates a character array, or string. The string is actually a vector whose components are the numeric codes for the characters (the first 127 codes are ASCII). The actual characters displayed depend on the character encoding scheme for a given font. The length of S is the number of characters. A quotation within the string is indicated by two quotes.

S = [S1 S2 ...]

S = [S1 S2 ...] concatenates character arrays S1, S2, etc. into a new character array, S.

Example:

%my simple string of hello world%

mystr = 'hello world';

disp(mystr)

This will display your string on command window.

tan(x) Tangent

acos(x) Arc cosine

asin(x) Arc sine

atan(x) Arc tangent

sign(x) Signum function

max(x) Maximum value

min(x) Minimum value

ceil(x) Round towards +1

floor(x) Round towards -1

exp(x) Exponential

round(x) Round to nearest integer

sqrt(x) Square root

rem(x) Remainder after division

log(x) Natural logarithm

angle(x) Phase angle

log10(x) Common logarithm

conj(x) Complex conjugate

abs(x) Absolute value

Now that we have studied about generating a string let's move towards its operations. What are the operations that are possible on string? We have complete list of operation that MATLAB provides us.

General functions related to strings that do not perform any major operations on strings are listed below.

Strings

"Help strings" displays the doc on strings provided by MATLAB

cellstr - Create cell array of strings from character array.

C = CELLSTR(S) places each row of the character array S into

separate cells of C

blanks - String of blanks.

BLANKS(x) is a string of x blanks.

deblank   - Remove trailing blanks.

R = DEBLANK(S) removes any trailing whitespace characters from string S.

Following functions are written to perform String tests.

iscellstr - True for cell array of strings.

ISCELLSTR(S) returns 1 if S is a cell array of strings else it returns 0. A cell array of   strings   is   a cell array where every element is a character array.

ischar   - True for character array (string).

ISCHAR(S) returns 1 if S is a character array else it returns 0.

isspace   - True for white space characters.

For a string S, ISSPACE(S) is 1 for white space characters else 0. White space characters   are   spaces, newlines, carriage returns, tabs, vertical tabs, and formfeeds.

Following are few of the String operations:

regexp   - Match regular expression.

S = REGEXP(STRING,EXPRESSION) matches the regular expression, EXPRESSION,   in   the   string, STRING. The indices of the beginning of the matches are returned

regexpi   - Match regular expression, ignoring case.

START   =   REGEXPI(STRING,EXPRESSION) matches the regular expression, EXPRESSION,   in   the string, STRING, regardless of case. The indices of the beginning   of the matches are returned.

regexprep - Replace string using regular expression.

S   =
REGEXPREP(STRING,EXPRESSION,REPLACE) replaces all occurrences of the   regular   expression, EXPRESSION, in string, STRING, with the string, REPLACE. The   new string is returned. If no matches are found REGEXPREP returns STRING   unchanged.

strcat - Concatenate strings.

T   =   STRCAT(S1,S2,S3,...)   horizontally concatenates corresponding rows of the character   arrays S1, S2, S3 etc. All input arrays must have the same number of rows (or any can be   a single string). When the inputs are all character arrays, the output is also a character array.

strvcat - Vertically concatenate strings.

S = STRVCAT(T1,T2,T3,..) forms the matrix S containing the text strings T1,T2,T3,... as rows. Automatically pads each string with blanks in order to form a valid matrix. Each text parameter, Ti, can itself be a string matrix. This allows the creation of arbitrarily large string matrices. Empty strings in the input are ignored

strcmp - Compare strings.

TF = STRCMP(S1,S2) compares the strings S1 and S2 and returns logical 1 (true) if they are identical, and returns logical 0 (false) otherwise.

strncmp - Compare first N characters of strings.

TF = STRNCMP(S1,S2,N) performs a case-sensitive comparison between the first N characters of strings S1 and S2. The function returns logical 1 (true) if they are the same and returns logical 0 (false) otherwise.

strcmpi - Compare strings ignoring case.

TF = STRCMPI(S1,S2) compares the strings S1 and S2 and returns logical 1 (true) if   they are the same except for case, and returns logical 0 (false) otherwise.

strncmpi   - Compare first N characters of strings ignoring case.

TF = STRNCMPI(S1,S2,N) performs a case-insensitive comparison between the first N   characters of strings S1 and S2. The function returns logical 1 (true) if they are the same except for letter case, and returns logical 0 (false) otherwise.

strread   - Read formatted data from string.

A = STRREAD('STRING')

A = STRREAD('STRING','',N)

A = STRREAD('STRING','',param,value, ...)

A = STRREAD('STRING','',N,param,value, ...) reads numeric data from the STRING into   a   single variable. If the string contains any text data, an error is produced.

findstr - Find one string within another.

K = FINDSTR(S1,S2) returns the starting indices of any occurrences of the shorter of the two strings in the longer.

strfind - Find one string within another.

K = STRFIND(TEXT,PATTERN) returns the starting indices of any occurrences of the string PATTERN in the string TEXT.

strjust - Justify character array.

K = FINDSTR(S1,S2) returns the starting indices of any occurrences of the shorter of the two strings in the longer.

strmatch - Find possible matches for string.

I = STRMATCH(STR, STRARRAY) looks through the rows of the character array or cell array of strings

STRARRAY to find strings that begin with the string contained in STR, and returns the matching row indices. Any trailing space characters in STR or STRARRAY are ignored when matching. STRMATCH is fastest when STRARRAY is a character array.

strrep   - Replace string with another.

S = STRREP(S1,S2,S3) replaces all occurrences of the string S2 in string S1 with the   string S3. The new string is returned.

strtok   - Find token in string.

STRTOK(S) returns the first token in the string S delimited by "white space". Any   leading white space characters are ignored. If S is a cell array of strings then the output is   a cell array of tokens.

strtrim   - Remove insignificant whitespace.

S = STRTRIM(M) removes insignificant whitespace from string M.

upper   - Convert string to uppercase.

      B = UPPER(A) converts any lower case characters in A to the corresponding upper case character and leaves all other characters unchanged

lower   - Convert string to lowercase.

      B = LOWER(A) converts any uppercase characters in A to the corresponding lowercase character and leaves all other characters unchanged.

We always need functions for String to number conversion.

num2str   - Convert numbers to a string.

      T = NUM2STR(X) converts the matrix X into a string representation T with about 4 digits and an exponent if required. This is useful for labelling plots with the TITLE, XLABEL, YLABEL, and TEXT commands.

int2str - Convert integer to string.

S = INT2STR(X) rounds the elements of the matrix X to integers and converts the result into a string matrix. Return NaN and Inf elements as strings 'NaN' and 'Inf', respectively.

mat2str - Convert a 2-D matrix to a string in MATLAB syntax.

STR = MAT2STR(MAT) converts the 2-D matrix MAT to a MATLAB string so that EVAL(STR) produces the original matrix (to within 15 digits of precision). Non-scalar matrices are converted to a string containing brackets [].

str2double - Convert string to double precision value.

X = STR2DOUBLE(S) converts the string S, which should be an ASCII character representation of a real or complex scalar value, to MATLAB's double representation. The string may contain digits, a comma (thousands separator), a decimal point, a leading + or - sign, an 'e' preceding a power of 10 scale factor, and an 'i' for a complex unit.

str2num - Convert string matrix to numeric array.

X = STR2NUM(S) converts a character array representation of a matrix of numbers to a numeric matrix

sprintf - Write formatted data to string.

[S,ERRMSG] = SPRINTF(FORMAT,A,...) formats the data in the real part of array A (and in any additional array arguments), under control of the specified FORMAT string, and returns it in the MATLAB string variable S. ERRMSG is an optional output argument that returns an error message string if an error occurred or an empty string if an error did not occur. SPRINTF is the same as FPRINTF except that it returns the data in a

MATLAB string variable rather than writing it to a file.

sscanf - Read string under format control.

[A,COUNT,ERRMSG,NEXTINDEX] = SSCANF(S,FORMAT,SIZE) reads data from MATLAB string variable S, converts it according to the specified FORMAT string, and returns it in matrix A. COUNT is an optional output argument that returns the number of elements successfully read. ERRMSG is an optional output argument that returns an error message string if an error occurred or an empty string if an error did not occur. NEXTINDEX is an optional output argument specifying one more than the number of characters scanned in S.

Chapter 12

Plots

Pictorial representation does have a high level of impact on any project. Plots are easy to understand. They help in making others understand the behaviour or output of project. You need not read the figure and then compare them, but just a simple plot can give the users complete and clear idea about the data. Trying to understand mathematical equations with graphics is an enjoyable and very efficient way of learning mathematics.

Let's learn how to Plot using MATLAB. MATLAB has many functions for generating plot and even customizing it adding a more professional look. Let's get started with a simple plot.

PLOT

Plot command generates a continuous line plot in new figure window.

Syntax

plot(Y)

plot(X1,Y1,...)

plot(X1,Y1,LineSpec,...)

plot(...,'PropertyName',PropertyValue,...)

plot(axes_handle,...)

h = plot(...)

hlines = plot('v6',...)

Description

plot(Y) plots the columns of Y versus their index if Y is a real number. If Y is complex, plot(Y) is equivalent to plot(real(Y),imag(Y)). In all other uses of plot, the imaginary component is ignored.

plot(X1,Y1,...) plots all lines defined by Xn versus Yn pairs. If only Xn or Yn is a matrix, the vector is plotted versus the rows or columns of the matrix, depending on whether the vector's row or column dimension matches the matrix. If Xn is a scalar and Yn is a vector, disconnected line objects are created and plotted as discrete points vertically at Xn.

plot(X1,Y1,LineSpec,...) plots all lines defined by the Xn,Yn,LineSpec triples, where LineSpec is a line specification that determines line type, marker symbol, and color of the plotted lines. You can mix Xn,Yn,LineSpec triples with Xn,Yn pairs: plot(X1,Y1,X2,Y2,LineSpec,X3,Y3).

Example:

x = 0:0.1:2*pi;

y =sin(x);

plot(x,y,'--rs','LineWidth',2,...

'MarkerEdgeColor','k',...

'MarkerFaceColor','b',...

'MarkerSize',5)

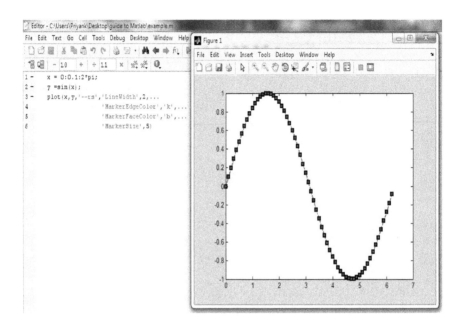

The above program shows the output as shown in figure above. The result of plot is always shown in a figure window. It is important to understand the functions available on figure window.

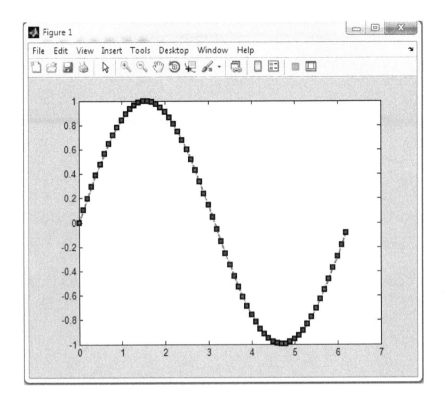

You may be able to see some basic features like zoom in or zoom out we all are familiar with their usage. Then there is option to print the plot. Then there are many more options that are available on figure window.

The various options as follows:

Legends

Link plot

Data cursor

3 D rotate

etc.

This was the simplest plot. Now that we have drawn a plot we need to add some helping text like x axis labels, y axis labels, title to the plot legends etc. to put all this MATLAB has provided us with functions.

Basic Plots and Graphs

axis

Axis scaling and appearance

Syntax

axis([xmin xmax ymin ymax])

axis([xmin xmax ymin ymax zmin zmax cmin cmax])

v = axis

axis auto

axis manual

axis tight

axis fill

axis equal

axis image

axis square

axis vis3d

axis normal

axis off

axis on

axis(axes_handles,...)

[mode,visibility,direction] = axis('state')

bar, barh

Plot bar graph (vertical and horizontal)

Syntax

bar(Y)

bar(x,Y)

bar(...,width)

bar(...,'style')

bar(...,'bar_color')

bar(...,'PropertyName',PropertyValue,...)

bar(axes_handle,...)

barh(axes_handle,...)

h = bar(...)

barh(...)

grid

Grid lines for 2-D and 3-D plots

Syntax

grid on

grid off

grid

grid(axes_handle,...)

grid minor

Description

The grid function turns the current axes' grid lines on and off.

legend

Graph legend for lines and patches

Syntax

legend('string1','string2',...)

legend(h,'string1','string2',...)

legend(M)

legend(h,M)

legend(M,'parameter_name','parameter_value',...)

legend(h,M,'parameter_name','parameter_value',...)

legend(axes_handle,...)

legend('off'), legend(axes_handle,'off')

legend('toggle'), legend(axes_handle,'toggle')

legend('hide'), legend(axes_handle,'hide')

legend('show'), legend(axes_handle,'show')

legend('boxoff'), legend(axes_handle,'boxoff')

legend('boxon'), legend(axes_handle,'boxon')

title

Add title to current axes

Syntax

title('string')

title(fname)

title(...,'PropertyName',PropertyValue,...)

title(axes_handle,...)

h = title(...)

xlabel, ylabel, zlabel

Label x-, y-, and z-axis

Syntax:

xlabel('string')

xlabel(fname)

xlabel(...,'PropertyName',PropertyValue,...)

xlabel(axes_handle,...)

h = xlabel(...)

ylabel(...)

ylabel(axes_handle,...)

h = ylabel(...)

xlim, ylim, zlim

Set or query axis limits

Syntax

xlim

xlim([xmin xmax])

xlim('mode')

xlim('auto')

xlim('manual')

xlim(axes_handle,...)

stem

Plot discrete sequence data

Syntax

stem(Y)

stem(X,Y)

stem(...,'fill')

stem(...,LineSpec)

stem(axes_handle,...)

h = stem(...)

hlines = stem('v6',...)

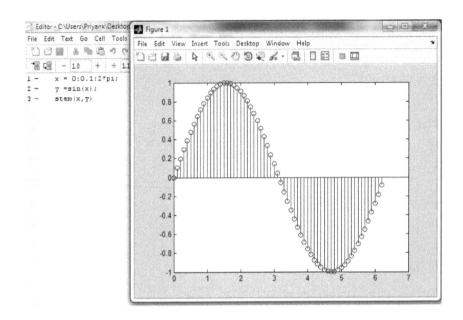

subplot

Create axes in tiled positions

Syntax

h = subplot(m,n,p) or subplot(mnp)

subplot(m,n,p,'replace')

subplot(m,n,P)

subplot(h)

subplot('Position',[left bottom width height])

subplot(..., prop1, value1, prop2, value2, ...)

h = subplot(...)

subplot(m,n,p,'v6')

Description

subplot divides the current figure into rectangular panes that are numbered row wise. Each pane contains an axes object. Subsequent plots are output to the current pane.

h = subplot(m,n,p) or subplot(mnp) breaks the figure window into an m-by-n matrix of small axes, selects the pth axes object for the current plot, and returns the axes handle. The axes are counted along the top row of the figure window, then the second row, etc.

Example:

x = 0:0.1:2*pi;

y =sin(x);

subplot(2,1,1);

plot(x,y)

subplot(2,1,2);

stem(x,y)

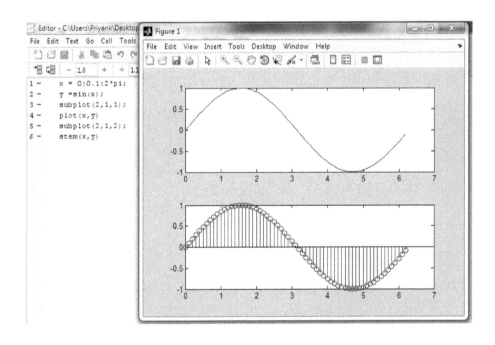

Thus the result of the program is only one figure window but two graphs in it.

Hold

If you continuously use PLOT without subplot then figure in figure window will keep on replacing and you will be able to see only the last plot figure. How to generate different plots?

To generate different plots we have to use Hold with following syntax:

Syntax

hold on

hold off

hold all

hold

We may require studying two or more entities simultaneously. In this case we may need to plot multiple entities in one plot with different colours, styles etc. You can refer the following example to learn exactly how to implement it. The following example also demonstrates many more function that we have discussed earlier.


```
x = 0:0.1:2*pi;

y = sin(x);

z = cos(x);

t = 0.01*tan(x);

plot(x,y,'--',x,z,'-',x,t,':')

xlabel(' 0 to 2pi')

ylabel('multiple plot')

legend('sin(x)','cos(x)','tan(x)')

title('my plots')
```

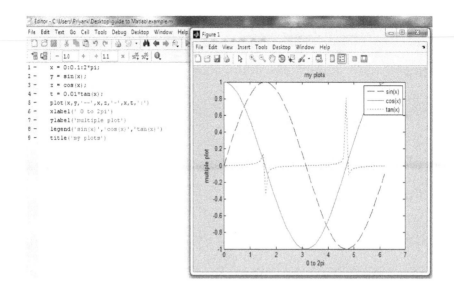

3d plot

Now that we have plotted our data in 2D plots we can move to 3D plots. 3D plots are really very cool and impressive way to present data. To plot 3D we have to use the following functions:

Plot3

3D line plot function that is able to plot in 3 axes.

Syntax

plot3(X1,Y1,Z1,...)

The plot3 function displays a three-dimensional plot of a set of data points.

plot3(X1,Y1,Z1,...), where X1, Y1, Z1 are vectors or matrices, plots one or more lines in three-dimensional space through the points whose coordinates are the elements of X1, Y1, and Z1.

plot3(X1,Y1,Z1,LineSpec,...)

plot3(X1,Y1,Z1,LineSpec,...) creates and displays all lines defined by the Xn,Yn,Zn,LineSpec quads, where LineSpec is a line specification that determines line style, marker symbol, and colour of the plotted lines.

plot3(...,'PropertyName',PropertyValue,...)

plot3(...,'PropertyName',PropertyValue,...) sets properties to the specified property values for all line graphics objects created by plot3.

If you see the logo of MATLAB even that is a 3 D plot. You can generate the logo using following code.

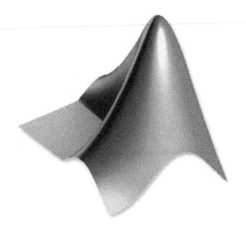

Code for logo:

L = 40*membrane(1,25);

logoFig = figure('Color',[0 0 0]);

logoax = axes('CameraPosition', [-193.4013 -265.1546 220.4819],...

  'CameraTarget',[26 26 10], ...

```
        'CameraUpVector',[0 0 1], ...

        'CameraViewAngle',9.5, ...

        'DataAspectRatio', [1 1 .9],...

        'Position',[0 0 1 1], ...

        'Visible','off', ...

        'XLim',[1 51], ...

        'YLim',[1 51], ...

        'ZLim',[-13 40], ...

        'parent',logoFig);

s = surface(L, ...

        'EdgeColor','none', ...

        'FaceColor',[0.9 0.2 0.2], ...

        'FaceLighting','phong', ...

        'AmbientStrength',0.3, ...

        'DiffuseStrength',0.6, ...

        'Clipping','off',...

        'BackFaceLighting','lit', ...
```

```matlab
    'SpecularStrength',1.1, ...

    'SpecularColorReflectance',1, ...

    'SpecularExponent',7, ...

    'Tag','TheMathWorksLogo', ...

    'parent',logoax);

l1 = light('Position',[40 100 20], ...

    'Style','local', ...

    'Color',[0 0.8 0.8], ...

    'parent',logoax);

l2 = light('Position',[.5 -1 .4], ...

    'Color',[0.8 0.8 0], ...

    'parent',logoax);
```

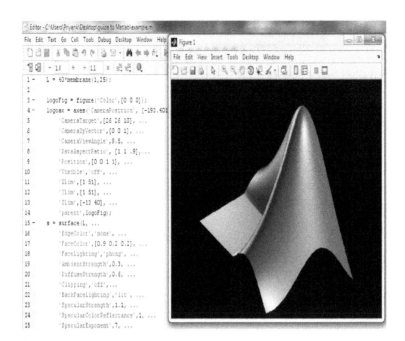

```
Editor - C:\Users\Priyank\Desktop\guide to Matlab\example.m

File  Edit  Text  Go  Cell  Tools  Debug  Desktop  Window  Help

                                                          Figure 1

                                                          File  Edit  View  Insert  Tools  Desktop  Window  Help

1 -    L = 40*membrane(1,25);
2
3 -    logoFig = figure('Color',[0 0 0]);
4 -    logoax = axes('CameraPosition', [-193.401
5          'CameraTarget',[26 26 10], ...
6          'CameraUpVector',[0 0 1], ...
7          'CameraViewAngle',9.5, ...
8          'DataAspectRatio', [1 1 .9],...
9          'Position',[0 0 1 1], ...
10         'Visible','off', ...
11         'XLim',[1 51], ...
12         'YLim',[1 51], ...
13         'ZLim',[-13 40], ...
14         'parent',logoFig);
15 -   s = surface(L, ...
16         'EdgeColor','none', ...
17         'FaceColor',[0.9 0.2 0.2], ...
18         'FaceLighting','phong', ...
19         'AmbientStrength',0.3, ...
20         'DiffuseStrength',0.6, ...
21         'Clipping','off',...
22         'BackFaceLighting','lit', ...
23         'SpecularStrength',1.1, ...
24         'SpecularColorReflectance',1, ...
25         'SpecularExponent',7, ...
```

Chapter 13

Graphics and Graphical User Interface Programming

MATLAB supports developing applications with graphical user interface (GUI) features. MATLAB includes GUIDE (GUI development environment) for graphically designing GUIs. It also has tightly integrated graph-plotting features. For example, the function plot can be used to produce a graph from two vectors x and y. The code:

x = 0:pi/100:2*pi;

y = sin(x);

plot(x,y)

Produces the following figure of the sine function:

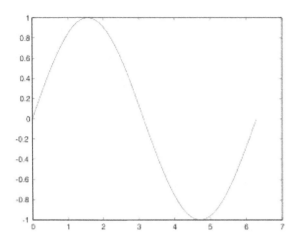

A MATLAB program can produce three-dimensional graphics using the functions surf, plot3 or mesh.

[X,Y] = meshgrid(-10:0.25:10,-10:0.25:10);

f = sinc(sqrt((X/pi).^2+(Y/pi).^2));

mesh(X,Y,f);

axis([-10 10 -10 10 -0.3 1])

xlabel('{\bfx}')

ylabel('{\bfy}')

zlabel('{\bfsinc} ({\bfR})')

hidden off

This code produces a wireframe 3D plot of the two-dimensional unnormalized sinc function:

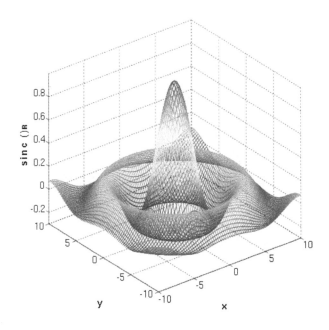

[X,Y] = meshgrid(-10:0.25:10,-10:0.25:10);

f = sinc(sqrt((X/pi).^2+(Y/pi).^2));

surf(X,Y,f);

axis([-10 10 -10 10 -0.3 1])

xlabel('{\bfx}')

ylabel('{\bfy}')

zlabel('{\bfsinc} ({\bfR})')

This code produces a surface 3D plot of the two-dimensional unnormalized sinc function:

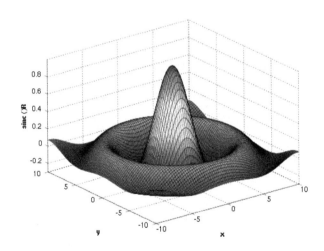

In MATLAB, graphical user interfaces can be programmed with the GUI design environment (GUIDE) tool.

Interfacing with other languages

MATLAB can call functions and subroutines written in the programming languages C or Fortran. A wrapper function is created allowing MATLAB data types to be passed and returned. The dynamically loadable object files created by compiling such functions are termed "MEX-files" (for MATLAB executable,] Since 2014 increasing two-way interfacing with Python is being added.

Libraries written in Perl, Java, ActiveX or .NET can be directly called from MATLAB, and many MATLAB libraries (for example XML or SQL support) are implemented as wrappers around Java or ActiveX libraries. Calling MATLAB from Java is more complicated, but can be done with a MATLAB toolbox which is sold separately by MathWorks, or using an undocumented mechanism called JMI (Java-to-MATLAB Interface), (which should not be confused with the unrelated Java Metadata Interface that is also called JMI).

As alternatives to the MuPAD based Symbolic Math Toolbox available from MathWorks, MATLAB can be connected to Maple or Mathematica.

Libraries also exist to import and export MathML.

Chapter 14

Autocorrelation using MATLAB

Here is a program for finding out Autocorrelation for a given signal. Autocorrelation is correlation of a signal with itself.

```
N=1024;

f=1;

fs=200;

n=0:N-1;

x=sin(2*pi*f*n/fs);

t=(1:N)*(1/fs);

subplot(2,1,1);

plot(t,x);

title('sinewave of frequency 1000hz');

xlabel('time,[s]');
```

```
ylabel('amplitude');

grid;

Rxx=xcorr2(x);

subplot(2,1,2);

plot(Rxx);

grid;

title('autocorrelation of sinewave');

xlabel('lags');

ylabel('autocorrelation');
```

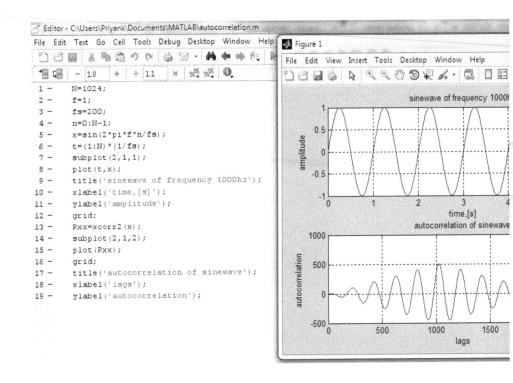

Advantages of MATLAB

- It has a solid amount of functions.

- MATLAB Simulink is a product for which there is no good alternative yet.

- It might be easier for beginners, because the package includes all you need, while in Python you need to install extra packages and an IDE.

- It has a large scientific community; it is used on many universities

Awesome MATLAB Tricks:

Batman Equation Curve in MATLAB: Copy paste the following code to get awesome batman curve.

here is a code "xr = linspace(-7,7,1500);

yr = linspace(4.5,-4.5,1500);

x = repmat(xr , [numel(yr) 1]);

```
y = repmat( yr' , [ 1 numel(xr) ] );


batman = (((x/7).^2.*sqrt(abs(abs(x)-3)./(abs(x)-
3))+((y/3).^2) .*  ...

        sqrt(abs(y+(3*sqrt(33)/7))./(y+(3*sqrt(33)/7))))-1)
.* ...

        (abs(x/2)-((3*sqrt(33)-7)/112).*(x.^2)-3+sqrt(1-
(abs(abs(x)-2)-1).^2) - y) .* ...

        (9*sqrt(abs((abs(x)-1).*(abs(x)-0.75))./((1-abs(x)) .*
(abs(x)-0.75)))-8*abs(x)-y) .* ...

        (3*abs(x)+0.75*sqrt(abs((abs(x)-0.75).*(abs(x)-
0.5))./((0.75-abs(x)).*(abs(x)-0.5)))-y) .* ...

        (2.25*sqrt(abs((x-0.5).*(x+0.5))./((0.5-x).*(0.5+x)))-
y) .* ...

        ((((6*sqrt(10))/7)+(1.5-0.5*abs(x)) .* sqrt(abs(abs(x)-
1)./(abs(x)-1))-((6*sqrt(10))/14).*sqrt(4-(abs(x)-1).^2)-y);
```

imagesc(log(abs(batman)));

"

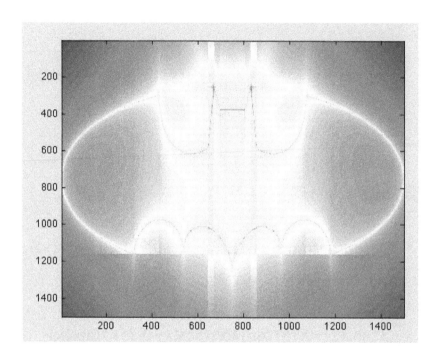

SPY

Put the "SPY" command in command window, it will create a spy image like this:-

The Conway's Game of Life

Yes, MATLAB can also be used to play games, enter the *Life* command and play.

The PENNY

This gives a 3D version of a penny.

Just enter "penny" command

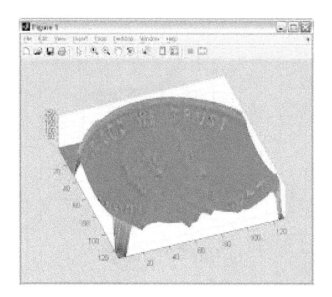

MATLAB PROGRESS BAR

Copy -paste the below code to get a progress bar:

```
clc;

clear all;

tic;

disp ('Hello, World!');

h=waitbar(0,'Please wait..');
```

```matlab
n=0;

for i=1:100

    waitbar(i/100)

    for j=1:100

        for k=0:100;

            n=factorial(2);

        end

    end

end

close(h)

toc
```

Please wait...

Chapter 15

How To Become A MATLAB Expert?

- MATLAB has one great feature that very few programming languages have: readable, comprehensive and accessible documentation. Use it! Search it simply using your favorite internet search engine. Practice browsing it via the hierarchical contents (which are all links), and understand how it is grouped by topic. Try the examples. Use the help to locate related functions and advice on how to solve particular problems.

- MATLAB blogs are an excellent source of inspiration and ideas. Loren Shure's blog is a mine of great ideas, and a veritable pleasure to read too.

- Breathe vectorized code, dream vectorized code and write vectorized code. Make vectorized code your first choice of problem solving, and leave those ugly low-level loops behind you... Understand why vectorized code is beautiful, and how it can be used to make your code much more efficient.

- And of course when loops are required, always preallocate the arrays before the loops.

- There are important ways to write fast and efficient code. Learn to use them.

- Learn good MATLAB programming habits right from the start, because life is too short to un-learn bad habits! This means: comment your code, use consistent formatting, write help (with H1 line) in every function, pass variables properly, use input checking, never use eval (or assignin, feval, etc), etc.

- Write functions, not scripts. Scripts are good for playing around, but not for real work.

- Refer to all graphics functions using explicit handle references (e.g. using Parent property). This makes plotting and handling figures much more robust and predictable.

- Pass variables reliably using input/output arguments (individually, in structures, handles, etc)... and avoid using globals.

- Imagine that every script and function you write is going to be given to someone else... impress them!

- Test everything thoroughly. Check each line as you write it. Does it really do what you think it is doing?

- Make a set of test-cases and collect all of the instances that fail while the code is being written, plus all the edge-cases and every case category that it needs to work with. You will not regret doing this!

- Break problems into parts, solve the parts separately. Make functions for code that needs to be repeated: this allows code to be reused, and bug-fixed in one location. Scripts are great for quickly testing an idea, but functions are much more robust for anything that will hang around for more than one day.

- Think about what you are doing. Actually think. What is the problem being solved? How can this be done? With what methods? Read Pólyas' excellent book How To Solve It. Don't get stuck thinking that you have found the best solution... there is often a better solution waiting around the corner, that just requires a new perspective.

- Check out other people's code on File Exchange (FEX). Note that the comments are often more useful than the ratings... and you will soon get an idea of whose comments are particularly worth paying attention to.

- Learn to use the debugging tools. These are indispensable.

- Practice!

****

Dear Reader, if you liked what you read, please leave an honest review in Amazon.

****

****

If you want to tell us about the quality or improvement areas in this book, please write to upskillpublishing@gmail.com

We read all your comments, feedback and inputs and ensure to make reading this book a pleasant experience by constantly updating it.

This guide is developed to help you to get started with MATLAB Programming. If we served this purpose, we consider it a success.

****

---The End---